One Unblinking Eye

One Unblinking Eye

poems

Norman Williams

Swallow Press

Ohio University Press

Athens

Swallow Press/Ohio University Press, Athens, Ohio 45701
© 2003 by Norman Williams
Printed in the United States of America

Swallow Press/Ohio University Press books
are printed on acid-free paper ⊗ ™

11 10 09 08 07 06 05 04 03   5 4 3 2 1

Library of Congress Cataloging-in-Publication Data
Williams, Norman, 1952–
    One unblinking eye / Norman Williams.
       p. cm.
    ISBN 0-8040-1057-9 (alk. paper) — ISBN 0-8040-1058-7 (pbk. : alk. paper)
    I. Title.

PS3573.I45515O54 2003
811'.54—dc21

2003042381

Acknowledgments

Poems in this collection have appeared in the following publications:

The Hudson Review:	"Games in the Darkening Air"
The Kenyon Review:	"Now, Until, Because"
	"An Invocation from the Hot Noon of Central Ohio"
New England Review:	"Taking Panfish"
	"Prayer for an Irish Father"
The New Yorker:	"A Christmas Song"

Contents

A Christmas Song   1

An Invocation from the Hot Noon
of Central Ohio   2

Now, Until, Because   3

Taking Panfish   5

Those Left to Tend   7

Coming to Terms   8

Prayer for an Irish Father   9

Portrait of Cecil Higbee   10

The Unearthing   12

Following the Crowd Home   14

Eastertide at Anse La Raye   15

Our Station   16

The Conversion near Jessups
on the Big Raccoon   17

The Doomsayers Awake Following
the Predicted Apocalypse   19

Independent Contractor   20

Horror at Hoosick Falls   21

Dispatch from Garelochhead   23

Near Antietam   24

Pegging Out   25

In Pavidus   27

From the Profound Ward   28

Nightwork   29

The Wrong Body   30

The Dow Is Off   32

Slave Ground near Pine Bluffs   33

October in the North   34

Words for a Young Widow in Maine   35

Prince Philip to Quit Exclusive Men's
Club Because It Serves Swan   36

Games in the Darkening Air   37

From A Journal of the Ascent   38

Delicate Repose   45

Farmhouse Left   46

One Unblinking Eye

A Christmas Song

Christmas is coming. The goose is getting fat.
Please put a penny in the old man's hat.
If you haven't got a penny, a ha'penny will do.
If you haven't got a ha'penny, God bless you.

Tonight the wide, wet flakes of snow
Drift down like Christmas suicides,
Layering the eaves and boughs until
The landscape seems transformed, as from
A night of talk or love. I've come
From cankered ports and railroad hubs
To winter in a northern state:
Three months of wind and little light.
Wood split, flue cleaned, and ashes hauled,
I am now proof against the cold
And make a place before the stove.
Mired fast in middle age, possessed
Of staved-in barn and brambled lot,
I think of that fierce-minded woman
Whom I loved, painting in a small,
Unheated room, or of a friend,
Sharp-ribbed from poverty, who framed
And fitted out his house by hand
And writes each night by kerosene.
I think, that is, of others who
Withdrew from commerce and the world
To work for joy instead of gain.
O would that I could gather them
This Yuletide, and shower them with coins.

An Invocation from the Hot Noon of Central Ohio

Off the interstate for gas in Marion,
Another town whose business district runs
These days to missions, adult films, and thrifts,
I watch the old emerge toward afternoon
To tend the hollyhocks beside garages,
Or budge their walkers down the buckled walks
With bags of vegetables. Inspecting belts,
The attendant tells of a farmer south of town,
Foreclosed, who last night set his house ablaze
With wife and son locked in. *Jesus,* he says,
Wiping his hands, and, nodding, I agree.
That oath stands in the heat that silvers from
The pumps and racks of tires for all that we,
As strangers, cannot say, about the clutch
Of banks and government, or of the way
That madness, without motive, creeps toward us
With music that is as singular and strange
As a glass harmonica's. I pay the man,
Decline my stamps, and nose the car once more
Past Cal's Roast Beef and Burger Chef. All day,
Between top-forty songs, I hear his half-
Hoarse voice come back, rising in the humid air,
Repeating that one word until it seems,
By turns, a muttered curse and stammered prayer.

Now, Until, Because

Today it is a summer dawn like that
Dawn seven years ago in Rome: a chance
        Of rain—not storms, but some
        Few drops that do not come,
Like a promise meant, but lost to circumstance.

We sat marooned inside the Stazione,
Just off the overnight. As morning set
        Its teeth, we waited for
        The cambio's barred door
To rattle up. It would be hours yet.

Beggars limped and shuffled past; a gypsy,
Scarved in satin, sold printed horoscopes.
        Outside, street vendors knocked
        Together stalls and hawked
Last Supper plates, or little plastic popes.

You traded cigarettes for Scorpio,
Then spoke the foreign words as if in prayer:
        "Adesso," "Fin," "Perchè."
        I utter them today
Once more, startling the English-only air.

A workman glances, wondering if I
Am to be feared. You said so, I recall,

But it was you in whom
The madness came to bloom
Like bitterroot. I did not guess those small

Affronts, imagined slights, or private moods
Warned of a crisis yet to come. A voice
That fall urged suicide,
And you, obeying, tried.
And then once more. In the end, there seemed no choice

But full-time care. At first, odd postcards came:
"My genes at birth were split and recombined.
Strange fingers start to grow,
And recent cat scans show
There is a tooth impacted in my mind."

Myself, I have become religious since:
At early Mass, I kneel in a middle row
And ask our Lord to spare
His mercy for your care,
Then, rising, suffer a mild vertigo.

Taking Panfish

Cedar Lake, Indiana

September now—the summer hordes
Have left this mudsink for their jobs
At stamping plants or salvage yards.
Unemployed, my father lobs
A worm and bobber out, then pours
An early drink. His idleness
Has its rewards. He tells of wars
Waged by the pike and small-mouth bass
That lurked here once, and as he speaks
My bobber dips, dragged bottomward
By unseen fear. A crappie breaks
The surface, flailing, hook set hard:
My father leaps up, yanks the rod,
And jerks the fish up past the rail.
"Keeper!" he crows, and I thank God
For not permitting me to fail.

Before my eyes, its stipple fades.
It gasps, but cannot catch its breath.
Wide-eyed and quivering, it bleeds
Behind the gills, then thrashes with
What seems a frantic, desperate
Resolve. My father, blade in hand,
Lays hold and bends to operate
To save the hook and leader. Stunned
And motionless, the crappie mouths

A final prayer which, if heard, is not
Allowed. My father whacks it, sheathes
The knife, then, squaring for a shot,
Flings it toward the Evinrude. All day,
As the fish grows slowly stiff and curled,
It fixes one unblinking eye
On me, as though I made this world.

Those Left to Tend

Across the bottomlands, the barns go down
Like fighters felled by one unlooked-for left:
They twist and stagger to the ground. Wash sags
Across the porches. Tractors, narrow-faced
And awkward as the men who drive them, peel
Back rinds of callused earth. Most now have quit
This place, that once had seemed so promising.
Each spring, abandoned orchards bloom across
The hills like lost ballets; clematis coils
Through old foundation stones, and, toward November,
Maples ignite beneath the black damp fog
Like candles at a vigil. The dead are there,
High-up, in hillside plots: confederates
Brought back in carts; miners, broken-backed;
And infants under unmarked stones, who died
Before their christening. They have the views,
Those sightless beings—they and those who tend
Them there, who lay bouquets or plastic wreaths,
The widows or the widows' only sons.
They are the left-behind, odd-mannered ones,
Who speak in starts, list when they walk; bereft,
In debt, in need of counterbalancing.

Coming to Terms

Come April now, he shirks the daily chores
And, taking up his rod and lures, sideslips
The bank near Claflin's Place, where Lewis Creek
Cuts through the field. The springtime flood there lips
A fissured granite shelf, and in its lee
Brook trout and speckled brown at evening break
The surface of the stream. It is his spot:
He wades thigh-deep, then dibs a jigger flea
To raise their ghostly trunks, but still, before
His cast is out, her image floats to view:
His infant, damp and shining, copper-new.
He lifts his arm half-up against the thought.

It was the doctor's choice, he thinks, yet knows
By keeping off and still, he also chose.
To let her go, that is. She dwelt apart
For seven months beneath a glass, hooked by
Electrodes to her charts, without sunlight
Or human touch. He signed at last. She died
Officially from a defect of the heart,
And yet her stunted ghost lives on inside
Some fold or recess of his mind. Each night
He hears her small, insistent voice ask why
She should have been conceived, just to decline.
Slipping, he sets his jaw, then gathers slack
Into his fist. All day, he works the line
In hopes a flash and strike will draw him back.

Prayer for an Irish Father

On a damp June Saturday, as colorless
As cellar stone, the working classes from
Dun Laoghaire spread their picnic blankets, tins,
And soda bread along the coastal cliffs.
Two hundred feet below, the ocean knocks
Debris and timber on the rock, and near
The precipice, I watch a father swing
His daughter out, as though to loose her on
That long descent, past rookeries of gulls
As intricate as mosques, through casual
Alliances of mist and fog, and toward
The cowlicked Irish Sea, as fathomless
And bitter as their history. With each
Return, the young girl cries out her delight,
Then girds once more against the peril there:
As though she knows no child is desired wholly;
That there is not a mother, dreading birth,
Who does not sometime curse her recklessness,
Nor father, yoked to press or forklift truck,
Who has not brooded on the chance of some
Untimely accident. Pray God that such
Black thoughts do not now reach like beggar's mitts
Into his mind, or better pray that he
Has vowed, despite them all, not to permit
His difficult and gnarled grip to give.

Portrait of Cecil Higbee

—An Historical Narrative

Pompadour'd and powdered, a forelock teased
By some stray rascal wind, he posed in Quaker
Finery before his carriage barn. Chin raised
And thrust, he seemed to tempt a haymaker
From Fate: say Poverty, or Dread Disease.

We bought his hundred-year-old portrait, hung
Slant-wise above the hearth, together with
The house and all its furnishings: ice tongs
And pick, cast-iron stove and clawfoot bath,
And each particular with something wrong,

Some wending crack, weak weld, or missing slat.
In those first months, we set about to brace
The sill and fumigate the attic bats,
Sure we had made a killing on the place.
The neighbors kept their views beneath their hats.

By slow degrees, we learned some fragments of
The local history: like puffs of cloud
Merino sheep once grazed the hills above
The town. Then came Collapse: Panicked Crowds
And Slaughtered Stock. Mills closed. Push came to Shove.

A cry rose up to root out Slavery,
And by that means to mend the woolen trade.

In vain: the farm fell into Penury.
Now, this fall, as the flame-stitched hills recede
To dour tweeds, and our spent century

Bumps and rattles to its end, I restore
Old Cecil to his former elegance
With solvent and a toothbrush. Noble sir!
Good soul! Would we could claim such confidence
And perfect poise, could dandify our hair,

Don riding boots, and promulgate our views
Through thick mustaches in rounded, walrus tones.
But here the postman, like a bargehand, tows
Winter closer behind each afternoon;
The shrew and fisher-cat increase; and crows,

At evening, mass like mourners in the town.
Rummaging through Higbee's barn a week ago
I came across a rope, dried-out and brown,
Cinched to a beam and frayed three feet below
The knot. Someone or thing had been cut down.

The Unearthing

July, 1991. "The fact of the matter is that a
rumor got started in Ekaterinburg that
Moscow had decided to open the grave and
take away the remains. And just as Ekaterin-
burg had not given up the Romanovs to
Moscow while they were alive, now they
decided not to give them up after their deaths.
Generally speaking, it was all identical: secret
murders and secret digging. Soldiers put a
barrier up around the work site and wouldn't
let anyone in. . . . They opened it up like
barbarians, without a priest. It was around
midnight when they came across the planking
Yurovsky wrote about. Then came bones and
entire skeletons, a skull with bullet holes and
traces of rifle butt blows."

—*The Last Czar,* by Edvard Radzinsky

Imagine Smorodin,
First Guard, a simple man:
Flat-nosed and sallow-faced;
Grown thick around the waist
From sausages and beer.
The place: a birchwood near
Ekaterinburg, the spot
Where Nicholas was shot
With family and train.
Past midnight now. Light rain
Tocks leaf to leaf to ground,
Like deadened chimes. A round
Praposhchik paces off

The site, then marks a rough
Bull's-eye. He indicates.
Smorodin nods. He weights
His spade, rocks back, and pries.
Two others do likewise.
His hundredth shovelful
Casts up the dirt-stained skull
Of Trupp, the children's stooge.
A worm, bewildered, huge,
Compresses and withdraws.
What if our hero does
Not sense the sudden flash
Of fatal shots; the gash
And thrust of bayonets,
Or little rivulets
And reservoirs of blood
Which briefly form to flood
Ipatiev's stone floor?
He was, as said before,
A simple man, not paid
To brood. He just obeyed,
No questions asked. But still,
He may have felt a chill,
As from a far-off scream—
And, later, he might dream
Of scattered teeth, like seeds,
Or how, before it bleeds
And clots, a bullet hole
Bores passage for the soul.

Following the Crowd Home

San Cristobal de las Casas

From the great parade and triumphant celebration
They pass into the poorer neighborhoods
Where shirtless children, not knowing what they face,
Play hoops and sticks around a broken fountain,
Then chase through reeking alleyways. The men
Fit keys into the doors of obscure shops,
With stock that no one ever seems to want—
Prosthetics, plastic urns, or plumbing parts—
Or else edge into dim garages, where
The hulls of cars wait for a missing valve
Or manifold. A tailor somewhere mends
A trouser leg, the whine of his machine
Rising to meet the drone of the cicadas
In the August heat. Before the Spanish court,
A lawyer drafts petitions for relief,
Unlikely as a prayer or lotto bet.
There will be war: the women are against;
The men and boys are for. That night the square
Is strung with bulbs. Children hawk cigarettes,
While couples dance to castanets and horns.
"Better to die on your feet than live on your knees,"
Some drunkard bawls. Police appear. Waists tight,
Backs straight, the dancers turn, and one sees then,
In each toe stamp, turn in, slide step and curl,
The gravity that causes them to whirl.

Eastertide at Anse La Raye

St. Lucia, W.I.

On this unclouded, humid Holy Thursday,
Within the unimposing, tin-roofed church
Constructed by the English, descendants of
The slaves have gathered, patient and erect
From bearing on their heads exotic staples:
The white dasheen, plantain, and passion fruit.
From the battered pulpit, an Anglican explains
The crown of thorns and tells of those oppressed
Two thousand years ago in Palestine,
Halfway around the earth. That afternoon,
The Easter sun swells and distends beyond
The wharves, where green bananas cling like young
To mother stalks. Later, as the jungle fills
With screeches, peeps, and chirrs, the villagers
Pass home to shacks or concrete cubicles.
One wonders, then, that they could bring themselves
To sing the hymns, consume the holy crust,
Or recognize in those who bound them here
A place for mercy, faith, or godliness.

Our Station

Stiff above the field's edge
The marsh hawk floats and winds.
Tuned to the slightest stir
Of milkweed stem or sedge,
It checks its flight to pitch
With talons spread, before
On backward-beating wings
It grasps a zagging hare
And rises, uttering
A shriek of joy in which,
Despite our doubts, we seem
To join, and in our minds
To clench our prey, and climb.

The Conversion near Jessups
on the Big Raccoon

On this moth-filled, dank Indiana night,
Inside the airless gospel tent, she recalls
Once more how delicate, how sparrow-light
Her father seemed when he had died. The shawls
And coverlets that weighed on him throughout
His year-long worsening were packed away,
And his curled body seemed almost to float
Upward into her arms from where it lay.

And so, she thinks, the preacher up on stage
Is right: our souls do have a heft and weight.
Blustering, bloodshot, his veins engorged with rage,
He rants that working stiffs and heads of state
Alike each lose ten ounces when they die.
Then, in a father's reassuring voice,
He adds that modern instruments don't lie.
We must believe. With Christ we have no choice.

Will there be witnesses? She draws a breath
And rises, filled with faith, to testify
About the odd particulars of death:
The jolt, and awful glazing of the eye,
As if the soul were simply gathered up,
Being called, as we are called, to serve our God.
The stagehands hustle out a banged-up cup.
The sweat-soaked followers of Christ applaud.

Outside, the crickets calculate the heat.
Against the tent, inflated shadows bow
And wave. She starts the car, awed by her feat,
Or, rather, by the certainty that now,
With Jesus Christ, her life at last must change.
Always, she hated what her father craved,
Her secret recesses of shame. Arrange
Yourself, she murmurs. Hoard what can be saved.

The Doomsayers Awake Following
the Predicted Apocalypse

This morning, after three full days of rain,
    The clouds lift slowly from the fields
Like lovers taking leave. The level sun,
    Obscured by trailing mists and vapors,
Whitens our soaking world of windrows, barns,
    And fence rails. Routines resume:
The neighbor's dog uphaunches and ambles toward
    A water pail. Last night, we saw
The blood-stained scimitar unsheathed and felt
    The wind of angels rushing past,
While Heaven flashed and thundered its command.
    Yet God today has stayed His hand:
Each bud and backward-bending stem of grass;
    Each droplet blurred by insect spawn;
And, aloft, a banking sparrow hawk held like
    A shining cross against the sun,
Bespeak a love too eager to forgive
    The blasphemers who mock His word;
The decadent, depraved, and dissolute
    Who squander His Son's sacrifice;
And those adulterers and sodomites
    Who do not seek the faith required
Each day to shame and mortify desire.

Independent Contractor

Forty degrees; the threat of rain. That time of fall
    When we are most inclined to end it all.
Denim-jacketed, with a faded sweatshirt hood,
        He draws his plane along a length of wood,
        Then takes a chisel to a cornice piece
        With two light taps. His movements never cease;
His cracked and callused hands, in gloves with fingers cut,
Rub up for warmth, then start like hares hawked by his thought.

He knows no other work; wants none. He learned this from
        His father—brace and auger, bob and plumb—
The same way he learned how to hunt or take a beating:
        Not by words but by a look, and by repeating
        Mutely each grimace, wince, set of the jaw.
        His job is more than workmanlike. No flaw
Or gap offends the eye. Each post and bull-nose stair
Seems proof of love—if love is proved by excess care.

Horror at Hoosick Falls

—A Criticism of the Cinema

Near the ruined tailrace,
Where the water, as though delighted still
By its foaming, lashing chase
Through fragments of the fallen mill,
Eddies beneath a row
Of swamp willows, the young boy spots
A murky stain below
The rippled surface, a crowd of blots
Like mercury, that parts, then forms,
Then parts again. He thinks he's found
A coat or bib, but never dreams
He's come across a woman drowned.
He notices the dangling sleeve,
Then sees a hump-backed torso heave
Slightly more slowly than a human breathes.
Close tight: a lifeless hand leaves water wreathes.

Dissolve. A beetle-browed detective
Combs through the underbrush, uncovering
A pair of pantyhose, defective
Pocket watch, key ring, and—strange—a string
Of hand-carved fetishes. Where these clues track,
Through what hedge-maze of high
Intrigue, I do not guess. My mind drifts back
To that bewildered child, just shy

Of puberty, who stumbled on the corpse:
What toadlike chill crept through his gut?
What sudden kinks, contortions, knots, and warps
Disturbed his panic-stricken thought?
Without jump cuts, soundtrack or visual effects
Could he conceive the killer's slowly stirring sex?
Or, imagining the victim's spasm of alarm,
Did he surprise his own peculiar urge to harm?

Dispatch from Garelochhead

The rough-edged, gull-gray clouds pass low across
The timber-littered coast, hauling cold rain
From Baffin Bay or Spitsbergen. On this,
Their final day, black-muzzled sheep emerge
And vanish in the fog. In lamp-faint light
That afternoon, the flock is herded by
A shepherd and his eager dog before
Each bleating tag is carted off to slaughter.
The job is solitary and obscure,
Yet in the nearby pub, among the men
Who now stamp chips or spot-check motherboards,
A few keep watch with half an eye, remark
The dog, its lift and fetch, as though such skills
Still mattered, as though aware, that is, of what
It means to work with death in every weather:
Cold, dank, raw, gray, and, rarely, beautiful.

Near Antietam

Shunning the British tourist bus, we walk,
My child and I, the West Woods where, like dogs
Who know their death is due, the wounded took
Themselves to give up hope. The horror begs
Imagining—the soldiers hauling limbs
Hacked off or messmates dead, and everywhere,
Mixed with the summer scent of swelling plums,
A stench of putrid flesh and burning hair.
Here Lee was turned. That night the forest filled
With muttered names of loved ones left, and cries
From mangled soldiers pleading to be killed.
Seeing my distant look, my daughter tries
My sleeve: "What is it, what?" she asks, and I
Say "nothing, nothing"—though "nothing" is a lie.

Pegging Out

Behind his kitchen chair, the drizzle gathers,
Slug-like, then slithers down the window. He cuts,
And deals, as though his bent, arthritic hands
Were engineered for it. At ninety-one,
His orbit's been reduced to table, stove,
And sleeping couch. "Will need a cut," he now
Announces, sloughing to the crib. I turn
A one-eyed jack for knobs, and we are off:
A fifteen-two, a go, a thirty-one,
It is a language used by whalers once,
By soldiers in their tents, and also by
My grandfather, who mastered idiom
And dialect while still a boy, confined
On winter nights to the one stove-heated room
on the far reaches of the unlit plains.

It is a game of getting round. We speak,
Between discards and counts, of climate change,
Prices of crops and politics, till on
The final turn he asks, "Hear from your dad?"
As one might ask a ballscore or the weather.
He means the man who ran out on his daughter,
Stuck him with debt, then every Christmas called
Collect from California. Nor does he want
An answer yet, but only means that we
Should think of him together, silently,

As we might pray, or watch TV. "Not much,"
I say at last. "Another game?" he asks.
I nod. It's raining still, and there is not
Much better left to fill his time. Nor mine.

In Pavidus

On this first small-leafed day of spring,
A mourning dove, like Jeremiah
Complaining in the limbs, starts with
His allah-hoo-hoo-hoo, and we,
Who came to celebrate, survey
Instead the winter's take. A rose,
Frost-blacked, does not send shoots. Nearby
A shagbark hickory extends,
Amid the early gold and green,
Three lifeless limbs against the sky.

How lightly we've escaped. No scare
Of cancer staggered our routine;
No madness mocked our courtesies.
I press my cold and cracking hands,
Not knowing if my nerves will hold;
Not knowing if my sins, by some
All-touching mercy, were excused
Or if, when brought at last to light,
Will bring the torment they deserve.

From the Profound Ward

Thick-tongued, agape, they lounge, sloth-still on chairs
Or chosen benches, heads hung or oddly cocked,
Or lolling slowly backward and around.
From time to time, their features shift, from dull
Despondency to a slow, dawn-breaking joy,
As if some single thought wound through their minds,
Illuminating, as it passed, huge hopes
Or dreamed-of kindnesses. Thus inward-turned,
They pass this last October day until
A patient, great with child, in circumstances
That neither she nor staff aides can explain,
Lumbers across the cross-cut lawn, and each
Turns dumbstruck, as in old Nativities
The rustics slowly turn, amazed, afraid,
Their most improbable imaginings
Borne out, by one both of them and beyond.

Nightwork

I heard them late, the traffic still, on summer nights
When windows stood thrown wide for any breeze
And sounds traversed the humid air like steel:
The couplings and uncouplings miles off
In Markham Yards, whose rails fanned beneath
Chicago ever outward to the South,
Like an ocean liner's phosphorescent wake,
Or so I, half-asleep, imagined it,
The rusted boxcars ramming hard against
The silver sub-shaped tankers, the sudden bang
And shudder lingering, or empty stocks
Like fragile skeletons being butted up
By hoppers mounded with bituminous,
The Soo Line latched to Erie Lackawanna,
Or Santa Fe to Chessie, and so all night
Until, near dawn, the freights were made and moved
By shouting men in gray-striped overalls,
Their bull's-eye lanterns waving "slow ahead"—
The very men whom I would later see
Off-shift, in early afternoon, emerging
From tar-bricked taverns near the tracks, or else
Outside the union local, pitching coins
Against a curb, as if, by day, they were
Reduced to ordinary men, or worse.

The Wrong Body

This afternoon, again, their faces flushed
From the double flight of stairs, the sergeants rushed
To my salon, held out the photograph,
And begged for me to "see." I had to laugh:
For all their labs, I was their last resort—
Zisska, once confidante to Lida's court
Of Thurn and Taxis: futures told, palms read,
And the dead evoked. As usual, I bade
Them fold their hands and sit like gentlemen,
While, peering in my crystal, I brought the scene
To view: a low-slung, brown-bricked neighborhood
Where once stockyards and slaughterhouses stood.

The spirit showed a two-room tenement
And, in the entryway, a pair of bent
And shattered bifocals, a mud-caked shoe,
Gold signet ring, and a billfold, rifled-through.
Against one wall, slack-jawed, face streaked with grime,
There slumped the listless victim of our crime.
Bloodstains had dried like lichen on his chin.
A film obscured one eye. His storm-dark skin
Had swelled until it seemed to shine. Enough!
There it is, officers, I said. Now off!
As usual, I waived my standard charge.
My policy, with murderers at large.

Imagine, then, when they came shoving back
That night to say I must have lost my knack:
They'd come up dry. Billy be damn. No shoe,
No ring, no spectacles. In short, no clue.
My doubts crept back, my secret fear that all
I had believed or seen within the ball
Were figments, wisps, or tricks—the flickering
Phantasma of my own imagining.
I felt the chill that those without my gift
Must feel at some disturbing dream or swift
Presentiment. Beware! All is not well!
And yet the grief to come no one can tell.

The Dow Is Off

Southbound, downwardly mobile in
A knocking ten-year-old LeSabre,
Totaled once and salvaged, rust
Gnawing at the rocker panels like
Fire at the curtains in a melodrama,
I imagine those for whom such news
Must matter: suave, smooth-featured types,
Untroubled by the odd details
Of racing forms or powerball,
Who, while I drove truck or counted stock,
Were wisely planning their estates,
Diversifying portfolios, or buying
A summer place with acreage.

Yet how their evening now is shot!
How flat the chardonnay, how bland
The tips of tenderloin must taste!
Of course, it's not the Dow alone—
The dollar's through the roof, T-bills
Have plunged, and, even now, the wife
Is pussyfooting at the club.
How birdsong-sweet and full of joy
Seems my life by comparison:
The Gulf's two hours off, where rigs
Pound at the solar plexus of
The earth, and where, on moonlit nights,
Perfumed mulattoes weave like snails
By the shore, leaving shining trails.

Slave Ground near Pine Bluffs

Upset and skewed by years of frost,
The peeling gate no longer closes.
Although the names are mostly lost,
One finds a lichen-blistered Moses
Or pitted Obadiah. Nearby,
Loblolly pines creak with the sound
Of empty greathouses. A dry
September cracks the red clay ground.

Odd afternoons, a woman, old,
Tent-dressed, with one good eye, adorns
The stones with beads, or strips of gold
And silver foil. Perhaps she warns
Night spirits off, or maybe guides
The Eye of God among the graves.
Once, while I watch, a pickup rides
Careening past. A finger waves:

A Southern welcome. I shudder at
The speed with which I've been found out.
A soft-shelled northern Democrat—
Unnerved, unsettled, undevout—
Who comes in hopes he might be blessed
By this bare plot, and by it changed;
Touched not by God but faith, expressed
In poor things, carefully arranged.

October in the North

With this first frost, the forest quickens—
The squirrels which, a month ago,
Had screeched and somersaulted trunk
To limb, now scratch the hickory
For nuts, like urchins desperate
From poverty. The final birds
Today start south. A fox, whose coat
On summer evenings gleamed among
The goldenrod, this morning strikes
A neighbor's coop and drags away
Its kill. There is a forest sense:
Some larger hand, once generous,
Is closing to a miser's fist.

Words for a Young Widow in Maine

The sinew of the hickory that grips
The axe, the rasp of salt against the skin,
Or rockbound earth that shines the steel plough
In spring, are thought along our coast to lend
A native character, though none can match
The force of grief: compare the fisherman's
Scored cheeks; the ligaments that rope the necks
Of lumberjacks; or the farmer's gnarled wrist—
Compare these with the widow's fisted look,
Then judge who has the most to bear. Think of
The ghost that each night slips between her sheets
Or of the sudden joy of being alone
Which troubles her for weeks. And you, who thought
Him mean, or too devoted to his drink,
Consider how the common fingerstones,
Bathed in the tidal slabs, grow luminous.

Prince Philip to Quit Exclusive Men's Club Because It Serves Swan

I saw them wild, unruffled and demure,
Drifting on a fouled creek in northern Cork,
Their grace and beauty disproportionate
To nearby rowhouses and package stores.
They seemed, therefore, a little out-of-date,
Like philology, or classical ballet.
Yet, reading of the prince's bold resolve,
I thought of them again, plucked, rubbed, and roasted
To a turn on platters decked with oranges,
Transported noiselessly through gilt-edged rooms
By swooping men in tails, then placed before
The aristocracy to quiet nods
And compliments. All this, today, the prince
Was giving up, as once, at Runnymede,
A former king relinquished certain rights
Of sovereignty. Tonight, so said the news,
The prince would dine in palace rooms on rack
Of Suffolk lamb, a Yorkshire pudding, peas,
Bouquets of broccoli, then, for dessert,
A simple dish, a trifle, say, or fool.

Games in the Darkening Air

Beneath the blue, metallic clouds of late
November, spotlit by the lowered sun,
The children die heroically. Shot down
In sprints across the lawn, they clutch their chests
And crumple, crying for life itself before
They still, sometimes with an emphatic twitch.
In that brief interval before they rise,
Reborn, and start for home, I picture them:
Heads tucked, close-quartered with the frozen ground,
Hearts pounding hard. Above, the oak leaves clatter
In the north wind, and, farther off, a stream
Of sparrows empties from a hickory
Like cinders from a flue. Then they are gone.
For hours, first. Then winter. Then, for years.

From A Journal of the Ascent

Breaking Camp

Shadowed on the two-man tent,
The leaves of aspen shift
And blur like quarters
In a riffled pool.
From a thousand feet below,
An updraft brings sweet news
Of sage and juniper.
A locust chirrs. Why rush?
And yet we shake our sleeping bags,
Knock down the tent, and thread
Our way through larch and lodgepole
Toward ice and knife-edged rock,
As though we could not be content
To age with grace
Or die with equanimity.

Weather Change

Last night, the wind turned
On itself and, like a tragic Greek,
Lashed the unloved and loved alike,
Raising hackles on the lake,
Wailing in high passages,
And stripping deadwood from the pines.
Rain followed until morning,
When we emerged into
A keener mass of air and saw
The mountain ribboned by new falls.
One thought of rooms
Filled with an unexpected music,
Or of an aging face
Transformed by some swift memory.

Toward Treeline

As we switched back, through smaller
And more gnarled firs,
The early-morning beings of fog
Skulked into the thinning air.
A roebuck, startled
From his standing sleep,
Hightailed through the underbrush.
At timberline, we came upon
The carcass of a savaged ram
And, beside a kettle, found
The flesh-hung bones of elk
Kept from foraging by snow.
Surrounded, now, by glaciers, bowls,
Streams and saddlebacks, we sensed
A law that, in its purity,
Would not admit of clemency.

Fall

Strewn across the mountain's flank,
Enormous boulders lay like loaves.
Staggered by top-heavy packs,
We worked and picked our way
Until, with one unholy crack,
A wedge-shaped stone came loose
And reared: Leviathan disturbed.
Upended, then, I sensed
The clutch of jaw and loins
That is instinct for the worst
And, landing in the sliding scree,
Took a rock across the jaw.
Awakening, unmoved, I gained
Myself by slow degrees,
Feeling first the sunlight,
Then the rise and fall of breath,
Then, at last, the ingrained ache.

Night Following

Tonight, burrowed in my mummy bag,
I catalogue my body parts,
Newly serious, like a widower
Struck by a winter flu.
My fingers chart out temple,
Lobe, ribcage, and jaw
With the half-familiar sense
Of absent residents returned.
The backpack's weight
Still haunts my shoulderblades;
My feet, freed of their boots,
Lodge in one another's coves
Like a couple from the hinterlands:
Shy, ill-shapen, and in love.

Camp at Thirteen-Nine

The creek that blazed our route
Lies stilled at twenty-two degrees,
And a final August light
Coruscates the ice. One hears
Complaints of rock being forced
By cold, and then only
The soundless zero of a place
Where zero has prevailed.

Blessing

Today the morning overcast
Gathers into scattered clouds,
Revealing our bare granite peak
Like a blackened Gothic spire
Thrust above a stone-walled market town.
We pass communities of marmots
At their obscure devotions,
While, beneath, the valley floor
Lies flecked: an Appaloosa's flank.
Scaling one last summit wall,
The mile-closer sun reaches deep
Within our necks and backs.
The day itself then seems
Like some true gift,
Unsought and undeserved,
Beyond our power to return.

Delicate Repose

The late September sun, in later afternoon,
    Was only faintly warm on their young skins.
The leaves, just dropped, or dropping still, had not begun
    To brown and curl. They looked no more than friends
Stretched side-by-each on the dormitory quad,
    Though her brown curls ambiguously fell
Across his outstretched arm. They spoke of what? An odd
    Roommate, professors odder still, until,
By slow degrees, their talking trailed off. As day
    Diminished into dusk, their drowsing bent
To languid dream; the summer slipped; and "like" gave way,
    Perhaps, to love. Their silent breathing blent
In rising bliss. Blood ticking to a single stroke,
    They seemed oblivious to any thirst,
Anxiety, or urge, until one stirred, which woke
    The other, who, by waking, woke the first.

Farmhouse Left

The trouble is, I think, as water floods
A bootprint left behind me in the mud,
That I would rather walk my troubles off
Than face them, one by one: repair the roof,
Remit the traffic fine, send out the damned
Apology. "O.K. Should not have slammed
Your kitchen door. Pathetic life. Or lover.
Behaved most boorishly. Forgive. Yours ever."

Why's that so hard? I wonder, clambering
Across a broken birch that blocks the path.
There's some would see it done all in a morning:
You know, the can-do types, successful, with
Attractive wives, wide lawns, homes on a tour—
And yet, for all of that, a little dense,
In that they do not seem to grasp the lure
In failure. Absurd! they snort. Makes no damn sense!

Whereas, myself, I grasp it in the bone:
The small, subversive thrill in letting phone
Bills slip, appointments pass, jobs slide until
Life starts its slow, tectonic tilt downhill—
And endeth here, where lives are scraped from sides
Of deer and garden plots; where double-wides
On concrete pads abut a hard-pan road,
And, in the hills, abandoned barns implode.

Back in, the road become a rivulet,
I stumble on a farmhouse left, it must
Be fifty years, untouched, with dishes set
And pans left out. A bathtub, black with rust,
Has crashed, claw-first, into the sitting room.
Mice skitter in the walls. A perfect cone
Of sawdust forms beneath a ceiling beam.
Vermin at work! The house is coming down.

What happened there, to interrupt their meal?
These northern woods, like families, conceal
All sorts of sordid facts and histories—
Was there a poisoning? Sudden disease?
A midnight flight from creditors? Or did
Some jittery recluse, joined to a cause,
Claim title to the place in simple fee
And shoot at any who might disagree?

On my way out, I check the local store
For some report on what it was that chased
The occupants away. "Gone since the war,"
The shopkeep shrugs. He is not one to waste
His words—a custom here, or ritual.
But why? The thought, it seems, has not occurred
To him before. "Nothing unusual,"
He says at last. "Or else we would have heard."

By which, I take it, he must mean the kind
Of facts which always win out in the end:
An eldest son gone off without a word,
A drought, or brucellosis in the herd.

Bad luck, and yet the sort that's bound to come
In fifteen years, or forty. Which shows that some
Mistake was made, a hope held out, or debt
Incurred, which, in the end, could not be met.

Now, like some shining logo of success,
A jet glints toward the pole, Paris-bound,
Or off for Rome, while I'm stuck on the ground,
A counterweight, fouled up and fortuneless,
To notice how the place slips into myth:
To watch roads rut, herds thin, gas stations close,
And to endure a time of year which those
Above would rather not be bothered with.

Here spring begins its slow, corrosive work:
A single drip, another, then a third
Drill cigarette burns in the snow. A bird
Bends to its business, like an office clerk.
The creek begins to quicken. Ice shelves retract,
While, deeper in, the high sun ulcerates
A frozen pond, until its center floats
Unanchored, like an old dog's cataract.